Contents

COUNTER-ATTACK
AND OTHER POEMS

BY

Siegfried Sassoon

TO ROBERT ROSS

Dans la treve desolee de cette matinee, ces hommes
qui avaient ete tenailles par la fatigue, fouettes par
la pluie, bouleverses par toute une nuit de tonnerre,
ces rescapes des volcans et de l'inondation entrevoyaient
a quel point la guerre, aussi hideuse au moral
qu'au physique, non seulement viole le bon sens, avilit
les grandes idees, commande tous les crimes--mais ils
se rappelaient combien elle avait developpe en eux et
autour d'eux tous les mauvais instincts sans en excepter
un seul; la mechancete jusqu'au sadisme,
l'egoisme jusqu'a la ferocite, le besoin de jouir jusqu'a
la folie.

HENRI BARBUSSE. (Le Feu.)

INTRODUCTION

Sassoon the Man

In appearance he is tall, big-boned, loosely built. He is clean-shaven, pale or with a flush; has a heavy jaw, wide mouth with the upper lip slightly protruding and the curve of it very pronounced like that of a shrivelled leaf (as I have noticed is common in many poets). His nose is aquiline, the nostrils being wide and heavily arched. This characteristic and the fullness, depth and heat of his dark eyes give him the air of a sullen falcon. He speaks slowly, enunciating the words as if they pained him, in a voice that has something of the troubled thickness apparent in the voices of those who emerge from a deep grief. As he speaks, his large hands, roughened by trench toil and by riding, wander aimlessly until some emotion grips him when the knuckles harden and he clutches at his knees or at the edge of the table. And all the while he will be breathing hard like a man who has swum a distance. When he reads his poems he chants and one would think that he communed with himself save that, at the pauses, he shoots a powerful glance at the listener. Between the poems he is still but moves his lips... He likes best to speak of hunting (he will shout of it!), of open air mornings when the gorse alone flames brighter than the sky, of country quiet, of his mother,[1] of poetry--usually Shelley, Masefield and Thomas Hardy--and last and chiefly--but always with a rapid, tumbling enunciation and a much-irked desperate air filled with pain--of soldiers. For the incubus of war is on him so that his days are shot with anguish and his nights with horror.

He is twenty-eight years old; was educated at Marlborough and Christchurch, Oxford; was a master of fox-hounds and is a captain in the Royal Welsh Fusiliers. Thrice he has fought in France and once in Palestine. Behind his name are set the letters M.C. since he has won the Military Cross for an act of valour which went near to securing him a higher honour.

Sassoon the Poet

The poetry of Siegfried Sassoon divides itself into two rough classes--the idyllic and the satiric. War has defiled one to produce the other. At heart Siegfried Sassoon is an idealist.

Before the war he had hardly published a line. He spent his summers in the company of books, at the piano, on expeditions, and in playing tennis. During winter he hunted. Hunting was a greater passion with him than poetry. Much of his poetry celebrated the

---

1   His father was a well-to-do country gentleman of
     Anglo-Jewish stock, his mother an English woman, a Miss
Thornycroft, sister of the sculptor of that name.

loveliness of the field as seen by the huntsman in the early morning light. But few probably guessed that the youth known to excel in field sports excelled also in poetry. For, in its way, this early poetry does excel. It was characteristic of him that nearly every little book he then wrote was privately printed. Poetry was for him just something for private and particular enjoyment--like a ride alone before breakfast. Among these privately printed books are Twelve Sonnets (1911), Melodies, An Ode for Music, Hyacinth (all 1912). The names are significant. He was occupied with natural beauty and with music. In 1913 he publishes in a limited and obscure edition Apollo in Doelyrium, wherein it seems that he is beginning to find a certain want of body and basis in his poems made of beautiful words about beautiful objects. Later in the same year, with Masefield's Everlasting Mercy (1911), Widow in the Bye Sheet (1912) and Daffodil Fields (1913) before him, he starts to write a parody of these uncouth intrusions of the sorrows of obscure persons into his paradise but half way through the poem adopts the Masefield manner in earnest[2] and finishes by unsuccessfully endeavouring to rival his master. In 1914 the War breaks out. Home on leave in 1915 he privately prints Discoveries, a little book which contains some of the loveliest of his 'paradise' poems. In 1916 the change has come. He can hardly believe it himself. 'Morning Glory' (privately printed) includes four war poems. He has not definitely turned to his later style but he hovers on the brink. The war is beginning to pain him. The poems 'To Victory' and 'The Dragon and the Undying' show him

---

2   I had this from his own mouth

turning toward his paradise to see if its beauty can save
him ... The year 1917 witnesses the publication of
The Old Huntsman.[3]
This book secured instantaneous success.
Siegfried Sassoon, on its publication,
became one of the leading young poets of England.
The book begins with the long monologue of a retired
huntsman, a piece of remarkable characterisation.
It continues with all the best of the 'paradise'
poems, including the loveliest in 'Discoveries' and
'Morning Glory.' There are also the 'bridge' poems
between his old manner and his new such as the 'To
Victory' mentioned above. But interspersed among
the paradise poems are the first poems in his final war
style. He tells the story of the change in a characteristic
manner--Conscripts (page 51, 'The Old Huntsman').
For like nearly every one of the young English poets,
he is to some extent a humourist. His humour is not,
however, even through 'The Old Huntsman' all
of such a wise and gentle tenor. He breaks out into
lively bitterness in such poems as 'They,'
'The Tombstone Maker' and 'Blighters.'

---

3   'The Old Huntsman,' Dutton & Co., 1918.

CONSCRIPTS

"Fall in, that awkward squad, and strike no more
  "Attractive attitudes! Dress by the right!
"The luminous rich colours that you wore
  "Have changed to hueless khaki in the night.
"Magic? What's magic got to do with you?
"There's no such thing! Blood's red and skies are blue."

They gasped and sweated, marching up and down.
  I drilled them till they cursed my raucous shout.
Love chucked his lute away and dropped his crown.
  Rhyme got sore heels and wanted to fall out.
"Left, right! Press on your butts!" They looked at me
Reproachful; how I longed to set them free!

I gave them lectures on Defence, Attack;
  They fidgeted and shuffled, yawned and sighed,
And boggled at my questions. Joy was slack,
  And Wisdom gnawed his fingers, gloomy-eyed.
Young Fancy--how I loved him all the while--
  Stared at his note-book with a rueful smile.

Their training done, I shipped them all to France.
  Where most of those I'd loved too well got killed.
Rapture and pale Enchantment and Romance,

And many a sickly, slender lord who'd filled
My soul long since with litanies of sin.
Went home, because they couldn't stand the din.

But the kind, common ones that I despised,
  (Hardly a man of them I'd count as friend),
What stubborn-hearted virtues they disguised!
  They stood and played the hero to the end,
Won gold and silver medals bright with bars,
And marched resplendent home with crowns and stars.

This book (in consequence almost wholly of these
bitter poems) enjoyed a remarkable success with the
soldiers fighting in France. One met it everywhere.
"Hello, you know Siegfried Sassoon then, do you?
Well, tell him from me that the more he lays it on thick
to those who don't realize the war the better. That's
the stuff we want. We're fed up with the old men's
death-or-glory stunt." In 1918 appeared 'Countermans'
Attack': here there is hardly a trace of the 'paradise'
feeling. You can't even think of paradise when you're
in hell. For Sassoon was now well along the way of
thorns. How many lives had he not seen spilled apparently
to no purpose? Did not the fact of war arch
him in like a dirty blood-red sky? He breaks out,
almost like a mad man, into imprecations, into
vehement tirades, into sarcasms, ironies, the hellish
laughters that arise from a heart that is not broken
once for all but that is newly broken every day while
the Monster that devours the lives of the young
continues its ravages. Take, for instance, the magnificent
'To Any Dead Officer', written just before America
entered the war. Many reading this poem would think

Great Britain was going to cease fighting. But nothing
of the sort. One must always remember that bitter
as these imprecations are against those who mismanaged
certain episodes in the war, the ultimate foe
is not they but the German Junkers who planned this
war for forty years, who have given the lovely earth
over to hideous defilement and the youths of all nations
to carnage...

Sometimes in this book Sassoon fails to express himself
properly. This fact is, I think, a tribute to his
sincerity. For his earlier work very clearly displays
his technical proficiency. But here what can he do?
Indignation chokes and strangles him. He claws often
enough at unsatisfactory words, dislocates his
sentences, tumbles out his images as if he would pulp the
makers of war beneath them. Very rarely does he
attain to the poignant simplicity of 'The Hawthorn
Tree' or the detached irony of 'Does it Matter?'

Can he then see nothing else in war? I remember
him once turning to me and saying suddenly apropos
of certain exalte poems in my 'Ardours and
Endurances': 'Yes, I see all that and I agree with
you, Robert. War has made me. I think I am a man now
as well as a poet. You have said the things well
enough. Now let us nevermore say another word of
whatever little may be good in war for the individual
who has a heart to be steeled.'

I remember I nodded, for further acquaintance with
war inclines me to his opinion.

'Let no one ever,' he continued, 'from henceforth
say a word in any way countenancing war. It is dangerous
even to speak of how here and there the individual
may gain some hardship of soul by it. For war
is hell and those who institute it are criminals. Were
there anything to say for it, it should not be said for
its spiritual disasters far outweigh any of its advantages.'

For myself this is the truth. War doesn't ennoble:
it degrades. The words of Barbusse placed at the beginning
of this book should be engraved over the doors
of every war office of every State in the world.

While war is a possibility man is little better than
a savage and civilisation the mere moments of rest
between a succession of nightmares. It is to help to
end this horror that Siegfried Sassoon and the many
others who feel like him have continued to fight as
after the publication of this book he fought in Palestine
and in France.

You civilized persons who read this book not only as
a poet but as a soldier I beg of you not to turn from it.
Read it again and again till its words become part of
your consciousness. It was written by a man for mankind's
sake, that 'that which is humane' might no more be an
empty phrase, that the words of Blake might blossom
to a new meaning--

Thou art a man, God is no more,
Thine own humanity learn to adore.

New York City,
Nov. 20th-23rd.
ROBERT NICHOLS.

PRELUDE: THE TROOPS

Dim, gradual thinning of the shapeless gloom
Shudders to drizzling daybreak that reveals
Disconsolate men who stamp their sodden boots
And turn dulled, sunken faces to the sky
Haggard and hopeless. They, who have beaten down
The stale despair of night, must now renew
Their desolation in the truce of dawn,
Murdering the livid hours that grope for peace.

Yet these, who cling to life with stubborn hands,
Can grin through storms of death and find a gap
In the clawed, cruel tangles of his defence.
They march from safety, and the bird-sung joy
Of grass-green thickets, to the land where all
Is ruin, and nothing blossoms but the sky
That hastens over them where they endure
Sad, smoking, flat horizons, reeking woods,
And foundered trench-lines volleying doom for doom.

O my brave brown companions, when your souls
Flock silently away, and the eyeless dead
Shame the wild beast of battle on the ridge,
Death will stand grieving in that field of war

Since your unvanquished hardihood is spent.
And through some mooned Valhalla there will pass
Battalions and battalions, scarred from hell;
The unreturning army that was youth;
The legions who have suffered and are dust.

COUNTER-ATTACK

We'd gained our first objective hours before
While dawn broke like a face with blinking eyes,
Pallid, unshaved and thirsty, blind with smoke.
Things seemed all right at first. We held their line,
With bombers posted, Lewis guns well placed,
And clink of shovels deepening the shallow trench.
   The place was rotten with dead; green clumsy legs
   High-booted, sprawled and grovelled along the saps;
   And trunks, face downward, in the sucking mud,
   Wallowed like trodden sand-bags loosely filled;
   And naked sodden buttocks, mats of hair,
   Bulged, clotted heads slept in the plastering slime.
   And then the rain began,--the jolly old rain!

A yawning soldier knelt against the bank,
Staring across the morning blear with fog;
He wondered when the Allemands would get busy;
And then, of course, they started with five-nines
Traversing, sure as fate, and never a dud.
Mute in the clamour of shells he watched them burst
Spouting dark earth and wire with gusts from hell,
While posturing giants dissolved in drifts of smoke.
He crouched and flinched, dizzy with galloping fear,

Sick for escape,--loathing the strangled horror
And butchered, frantic gestures of the dead.

An officer came blundering down the trench:
"Stand-to and man the fire-step!" On he went ...
Gasping and bawling, "Fire-step ... counter-attack!"
   Then the haze lifted. Bombing on the right
   Down the old sap: machine-guns on the left;
   And stumbling figures looming out in front.
   "O Christ, they're coming at us!" Bullets spat,
And he remembered his rifle ... rapid fire ...

And started blazing wildly ... then a bang
Crumpled and spun him sideways, knocked him out
To grunt and wriggle: none heeded him; he choked
And fought the flapping veils of smothering gloom,
Lost in a blurred confusion of yells and groans ...
Down, and down, and down, he sank and drowned,
Bleeding to death. The counter-attack had failed.

THE REAR-GUARD
(Hindenburg Line, April 1917.)

Groping along the tunnel, step by step,
He winked his prying torch with patching glare
From side to side, and sniffed the unwholesome air.

Tins, boxes, bottles, shapes too vague to know,
A mirror smashed, the mattress from a bed;
And he, exploring fifty feet below
The rosy gloom of battle overhead.

Tripping, he grabbed the wall; saw some one lie
Humped at his feet, half-hidden by a rug,
And stooped to give the sleeper's arm a tug.
"I'm looking for headquarters." No reply.
"God blast your neck!" (For days he'd had no sleep.)
"Get up and guide me through this stinking place."
Savage, he kicked a soft, unanswering heap,
And flashed his beam across the livid face
Terribly glaring up, whose eyes yet wore
Agony dying hard ten days before;
And fists of fingers clutched a blackening wound.

Alone he staggered on until he found
Dawn's ghost that filtered down a shafted stair
To the dazed, muttering creatures underground

Who hear the boom of shells in muffled sound.
At last, with sweat of horror in his hair,
He climbed through darkness to the twilight air,
Unloading hell behind him step by step.

WIRERS

"Pass it along, the wiring party's going out"--
And yawning sentries mumble, "Wirers going out,"
Unravelling; twisting; hammering stakes with muffled thud,
They toil with stealthy haste and anger in their blood.

The Boche sends up a flare. Black forms stand rigid there,
Stock-still like posts; then darkness, and the clumsy ghosts
Stride hither and thither, whispering, tripped by clutching snare
Of snags and tangles.
          Ghastly dawn with vaporous coasts
Gleams desolate along the sky, night's misery ended.

Young Hughes was badly hit; I heard him carried away,
Moaning at every lurch; no doubt he'll die to-day.
But *we* can say the front-line wire's been safely mended.

ATTACK

At dawn the ridge emerges massed and dun
In the wild purple of the glowering sun,
Smouldering through spouts of drifting smoke that shroud
The menacing scarred slope; and, one by one,
Tanks creep and topple forward to the wire.
The barrage roars and lifts. Then, clumsily bowed
With bombs and guns and shovels and battle-gear,
Men jostle and climb to meet the bristling fire.
Lines of grey, muttering faces, masked with fear,
They leave their trenches, going over the top,
While time ticks blank and busy on their wrists,
And hope, with furtive eyes and grappling fists,
Flounders in mud. O Jesu, make it stop!

DREAMERS

Soldiers are citizens of death's grey land,
  Drawing no dividend from time's to-morrows.
In the great hour of destiny they stand,
  Each with his feuds, and jealousies, and sorrows.
Soldiers are sworn to action; they must win
  Some flaming, fatal climax with their lives.
Soldiers are dreamers; when the guns begin
  They think of firelit homes, clean beds, and wives.

I see them in foul dug-outs, gnawed by rats,
  And in the ruined trenches, lashed with rain,
Dreaming of things they did with balls and bats,
  And mocked by hopeless longing to regain
Bank-holidays, and picture shows, and spats,
  And going to the office in the train.

HOW TO DIE

Dark clouds aresmouldering into red
  While down the craters morning burns.
The dying soldier shifts his head
  To watch the glory that returns:
He lifts his fingers toward the skies
  Where holy brightness breaks in flame;
Radiance reflected in his eyes,
  And on his lips a whispered name.

You'd think, to hear some people talk,
  That lads go West with sobs and curses,
And sullen faces white as chalk,
  Hankering for wreaths and tombs and hearses.
But they've been taught the way to do it
  Like Christian soldiers; not with haste
And shuddering groans; but passing through it
  With due regard for decent taste.

THE EFFECT

"The effect of our bombardment was terrific. One man
told me he had never seen so many dead before."-- **War Correspondent**.

"He'd never seen so many dead before."
They sprawled in yellow daylight while he swore
And gasped and lugged his everlasting load
Of bombs along what once had been a road.
"How peaceful are the dead."
Who put that silly gag in some one's head?

"He'd never seen so many dead before."
The lilting words danced up and down his brain,
While corpses jumped and capered in the rain.
No, no; he wouldn't count them any more ...
The dead have done with pain:
They've choked; they can't come back to life again.

When Dick was killed last week he looked like that,
Flapping along the fire-step like a fish,
After the blazing crump had knocked him flat ...
"How many dead? As many as ever you wish.
Don't count 'em; they're too many.
Who'll buy my nice fresh corpses, two a penny?"

TWELVE MONTHS AFTER

Hullo! here's my platoon, the lot I had last year.
"The war'll be over soon."
        "What 'opes?"
          "No bloody fear!"
Then, "Number Seven, 'shun! All present and correct."
They're standing in the sun, impassive and erect.
Young Gibson with his grin; and Morgan, tired and white;
Jordan, who's out to win a D.C.M. some night;
And Hughes that's keen on wiring; and Davies ('79),
Who always must be firing at the Boche front line.

         *   *   *   *   *

"Old soldiers never die; they simply fide a-why!"
That's what they used to sing along the roads last spring;
That's what they used to say before the push began;
That's where they are to-day, knocked over to a man.

THE FATHERS

Snug at the club two fathers sat,
Gross, goggle-eyed, and full of chat.
One of them said: "My eldest lad
Writes cheery letters from Bagdad.
But Arthur's getting all the fun
At Arras with his nine-inch gun."

"Yes," wheezed the other, "that's the luck!
My boy's quite broken-hearted, stuck
In England training all this year.
Still, if there's truth in what we hear,
The Huns intend to ask for more
  Before they bolt across the Rhine."
I watched them toddle through the door--
  These impotent old friends of mine.

BASE DETAILS

If I were fierce, and bald, and short of breath,
  I'd live with scarlet Majors at the Base,
d to know his father well;
  Yes, we've lost heavily in this last scrap."
And when the war is done and youth stone dead,
  I'd toddle safely home and die--in bed.

THE GENERAL

"Good-morning; good-morning!" the General said
When we met him last week on our way to the line.
Now the soldiers he smiled at are most of 'em dead,
And we're cursing his staff for incompetent swine.
"He's a cheery old card," grunted Harry to Jack
As they slogged up to Arras with rifle and pack.

*   *   *   *   *

But he did for them both by his plan of attack.

LAMENTATIONS

I found him in the guard-room at the Base.
From the blind darkness I had heard his crying
And blundered in. With puzzled, patient face
A sergeant watched him; it was no good trying
To stop it; for he howled and beat his chest.
And, all because his brother had gone West,
Raved at the bleeding war; his rampant grief
Moaned, shouted, sobbed, and choked, while he was kneeling
Half-naked on the floor. In my belief
Such men have lost all patriotic feeling.

DOES IT MATTER?

Does it matter?--losing your leg? ...
For people will always be kind,
And you need not show that you mind
When the others come in after hunting
To gobble their muffins and eggs.

Does it matter?--losing your sight? ...
There's such splendid work for the blind;
And people will always be kind,
As you sit on the terrace remembering
And turning your face to the light.

Do they matter?--those dreams from the pit? ...
You can drink and forget and be glad,
And people won't say that you're mad;
For they'll know that you've fought for your country,
And no one will worry a bit.

FIGHT TO A FINISH

The boys came back. Bands played and flags were flying,
  And Yellow-Pressmen thronged the sunlit street
To cheer the soldiers who'd refrained from dying,
  And hear the music of returning feet.
"Of all the thrills and ardours War has brought,
  This moment is the finest." (So they thought.)

Snapping their bayonets on to charge the mob,
  Grim Fusiliers broke ranks with glint of steel.
At last the boys had found a cushy job.

*   *   *   *   *

  I heard the Yellow-Pressmen grunt and squeal;
And with my trusty bombers turned and went
To clear those Junkers out of Parliament.

EDITORIAL IMPRESSIONS

He seemed so certain "all was going well,"
As he discussed the glorious time he'd had
While visiting the trenches.
                    "One can tell
You've gathered big impressions!" grinned the lad
Who'd been severely wounded in the back
In some wiped-out impossible Attack.
"Impressions? Yes, most vivid! I am writing
A little book called **Europe on the Rack**,
Based on notes made while witnessing the fighting.
I hope I've caught the feeling of 'the Line'
And the amazing spirit of the troops.
By Jove, those flying-chaps of ours are fine!
I watched one daring beggar looping loops,
Soaring and diving like some bird of prey.
And through it all I felt that splendour shine
Which makes us win."
              The soldier sipped his wine.
"Ah, yes, but it's the Press that leads the way!"

SUICIDE IN THE TRENCHES

I knew a simple soldier boy
Who grinned at life in empty joy,
Slept soundly through the lonesome dark,
And whistled early with the lark.

In winter trenches, cowed and glum,
With crumps and lice and lack of rum,
He put a bullet through his brain.
No one spoke of him again.

   * * * * *

You snug-faced crowds with kindling eye
Who cheer when soldier lads march by,
Sneak home and pray you'll never know
The hell where youth and laughter go.

GLORY OF WOMEN

You love us when we're heroes, home on leave,
Or wounded in a mentionable place.
You worship decorations; you believe
That chivalry redeems the war's disgrace.
You make us shells. You listen with delight,
By tales of dirt and danger fondly thrilled.
You crown our distant ardours while we fight,
And mourn our laurelled memories when we're killed.
You can't believe that British troops "retire"
When hell's last horror breaks them, and they run,
Trampling the terrible corpses--blind with blood.
  O German mother dreaming by the fire,
  While you are knitting socks to send your son
  His face is trodden deeper in the mud.

THEIR FRAILTY

He's got a Blighty wound. He's safe; and then
  War's fine and bold and bright.
She can forget the doomed and prisoned men
  Who agonize and fight.

He's back in France. She loathes the listless strain
  And peril of his plight.
Beseeching Heaven to send him home again,
  She prays for peace each night.

Husbands and sons and lovers; everywhere
  They die; War bleeds us white.
Mothers and wives and sweethearts,--they don't care
  So long as He's all right.

THE HAWTHORN TREE

Not much to me is yonder lane
  Where I go every day;
But when there's been a shower of rain
  And hedge-birds whistle gay,
I know my lad that's out in France
  With fearsome things to see
Would give his eyes for just one glance
  At our white hawthorn tree.

            *   *   *   *   *

Not much to me is yonder lane
  Where *he* so longs to tread;
But when there's been a shower of rain
I think I'll never weep again
  Until I've heard he's dead.

THE INVESTITURE

God with a Roll of Honour in His hand
Sits welcoming the heroes who have died,
While sorrowless angels ranked on either side
Stand easy in Elysium's meadow-land.
Then *you* come shyly through the garden gate,
Wearing a blood-soaked bandage on your head;
And God says something kind because you're dead,
And homesick, discontented with your fate.

If I were there we'd snowball Death with skulls;
Or ride away to hunt in Devil's Wood
With ghosts of puppies that we walked of old.
But you're alone; and solitude annuls
Our earthly jokes; and strangely wise and good
You roam forlorn along the streets of gold.

TRENCH DUTY

Shaken from sleep, and numbed and scarce awake,
Out in the trench with three hours' watch to take,
I blunder through the splashing mirk; and then
Hear the gruff muttering voices of the men
Crouching in cabins candle-chinked with light.
Hark! There's the big bombardment on our right
Rumbling and bumping; and the dark's a glare
Of flickering horror in the sectors where
We raid the Boche; men waiting, stiff and chilled,
Or crawling on their bellies through the wire.
"What? Stretcher-bearers wanted? Some one killed?"
Five minutes ago I heard a sniper fire:
Why did he do it? ... Starlight overhead--
Blank stars. I'm wide-awake; and some chap's dead.

BREAK OF DAY

There seemed a smell of autumn in the air
At the bleak end of night; he shivered there
In a dank, musty dug-out where he lay,
Legs wrapped in sand-bags,--lumps of chalk and clay
Spattering his face. Dry-mouthed, he thought, "To-day
We start the damned attack; and, Lord knows why,
Zero's at nine; how bloody if I'm done in
Under the freedom of that morning sky!"
And then he coughed and dozed, cursing the din.

Was it the ghost of autumn in that smell
Of underground, or God's blank heart grown kind,
That sent a happy dream to him in hell?--
Where men are crushed like clods, and crawl to find
Some crater for their wretchedness; who lie
In outcast immolation, doomed to die
Far from clean things or any hope of cheer,
Cowed anger in their eyes, till darkness brims
And roars into their heads, and they can hear
Old childish talk, and tags of foolish hymns.

He sniffs the chilly air; (his dreaming starts).
He's riding in a dusty Sussex lane
In quiet September; slowly night departs;

And he's a living soul, absolved from pain.
Beyond the brambled fences where he goes
Are glimmering fields with harvest piled in sheaves,
And tree-tops dark against the stars grown pale;
Then, clear and shrill, a distant farm-cock crows;
And there's a wall of mist along the vale
Where willows shake their watery-sounding leaves.
He gazes on it all, and scarce believes
That earth is telling its old peaceful tale;
He thanks the blessed world that he was born ...
Then, far away, a lonely note of the horn.

They're drawing the Big Wood! Unlatch the gate,
And set Golumpus going on the grass:
He knows the corner where it's best to wait
And hear the crashing woodland chorus pass;
The corner where old foxes make their track
To the Long Spinney; that's the place to be.
The bracken shakes below an ivied tree,
And then a cub looks out; and "Tally-o-back!"
He bawls, and swings his thong with volleying crack,--
All the clean thrill of autumn in his blood,
And hunting surging through him like a flood
In joyous welcome from the untroubled past;
While the war drifts away, forgotten at last.

Now a red, sleepy sun above the rim
Of twilight stares along the quiet weald,
And the kind, simple country shines revealed
In solitudes of peace, no longer dim.
The old horse lifts his face and thanks the light,
Then stretches down his head to crop the green.
All things that he has loved are in his sight;

The places where his happiness has been
Are in his eyes, his heart, and they are good.

       *   *   *   *   *

Hark! there's the horn: they're drawing the Big Wood.

TO ANY DEAD OFFICER

Well, how are things in Heaven? I wish you'd say,
  Because I'd like to know that you're all right.
Tell me, have you found everlasting day,
  Or been sucked in by everlasting night?
For when I shut my eyes your face shows pain;
  I hear you make some cheery old remark--
I can rebuild you in my brain,
  Though you've gone out patrolling in the dark.

You hated tours of trenches; you were proud
  Of nothing more than having good years to spend;
Longed to get home and join the careless crowd
  Of chaps who work in peace with Time for friend.
That's all washed out now. You're beyond the wire:
  No earthly chance can send you crawling back;
You've finished with machine-gun fire--
Knocked over in a hopeless dud-attack.

Somehow I always thought you'd get done in,
  Because you were so desperate keen to live:
You were all out to try and save your skin,
  Well knowing how much the world had got to give.
You joked at shells and talked the usual "shop,"
  Stuck to your dirty job and did it fine:

With "Jesus Christ! when *will* it stop?
Three years... It's hell unless we break their line."

So when they told me you'd been left for dead
  I wouldn't believe them, feeling it *must* be true.
Next week the bloody Roll of Honour said
  "Wounded and missing"--(That's the thing to do
When lads are left in shell-holes dying slow,
  With nothing but blank sky and wounds that ache,
Moaning for water till they know
  It's night, and then it's not worth while to wake!)

          *   *   *   *   *

Good-bye, old lad! Remember me to God,
  And tell Him that our Politicians swear
They won't give in till Prussian Rule's been trod
  Under the Heel of England... Are you there? ...
Yes ... and the War won't end for at least two years;
But we've got stacks of men... I'm blind with tears,
  Staring into the dark. Cheero!
I wish they'd killed you in a decent show.

SICK LEAVE

When I'm asleep, dreaming and lulled and warm,--
They come, the homeless ones, the noiseless dead.
While the dim charging breakers of the storm
Bellow and drone and rumble overhead,
Out of the gloom they gather about my bed.
  They whisper to my heart; their thoughts are mine.
  "Why are you here with all your watches ended?
  From Ypres to Frise we sought you in the Line."
In bitter safety I awake, unfriended;
And while the dawn begins with slashing rain
I think of the Battalion in the mud.
"When are you going out to them again?
Are they not still your brothers through our blood?"

BANISHMENT

I am banished from the patient men who fight.
They smote my heart to pity, built my pride.
Shoulder to aching shoulder, side by side,
They trudged away from life's broad wealds of light.
Their wrongs were mine; and ever in my sight
They went arrayed in honour. But they died,--
Not one by one: and mutinous I cried
To those who sent them out into the night.

The darkness tells how vainly I have striven
To free them from the pit where they must dwell
In outcast gloom convulsed and jagged and riven
By grappling guns. Love drove me to rebel.
Love drives me back to grope with them through hell;
And in their tortured eyes I stand forgiven.

SONG-BOOKS OF THE WAR

In fifty years, when peace outshines
Remembrance of the battle lines,
Adventurous lads will sigh and cast
Proud looks upon the plundered past.
On summer morn or winter's night,
Their hearts will kindle for the fight,
Reading a snatch of soldier-song,
Savage and jaunty, fierce and strong;
And through the angry marching rhymes
Of blind regret and haggard mirth,
They'll envy us the dazzling times
When sacrifice absolved our earth.
Some ancient man with silver locks
Will lift his weary face to say:
"War was a fiend who stopped our clocks
Although we met him grim and gay."
And then he'll speak of Haig's last drive,
Marvelling that any came alive
Out of the shambles that men built
And smashed, to cleanse the world of guilt.
But the boys, with grin and sidelong glance,
Will think, "Poor grandad's day is done."
And dream of those who fought in France
And lived in time to share the fun.

THRUSHES

Tossed on the glittering air they soar and skim,
Whose voices make the emptiness of light
A windy palace. Quavering from the brim
Of dawn, and bold with song at edge of night,
They clutch their leafy pinnacles and sing
Scornful of man, and from his toils aloof
Whose heart's a haunted woodland whispering;
Whose thoughts return on tempest-baffled wing;
Who hears the cry of God in everything,
And storms the gate of nothingness for proof.

AUTUMN

October's bellowing anger breaks and cleaves
The bronzed battalions of the stricken wood
In whose lament I hear a voice that grieves
For battle's fruitless harvest, and the feud
Of outraged men. Their lives are like the leaves
Scattered in flocks of ruin, tossed and blown
Along the westering furnace flaring red.
O martyred youth and manhood overthrown,
The burden of your wrongs is on my head.

INVOCATION

Come down from heaven to meet me when my breath
Chokes, and through drumming shafts of stifling death
I stumble toward escape, to find the door
Opening on morn where I may breathe once more
Clear cock-crow airs across some valley dim
With whispering trees. While dawn along the rim
Of night's horizon flows in lakes of fire,
Come down from heaven's bright hill, my song's desire.

Belov'd and faithful, teach my soul to wake
In glades deep-ranked with flowers that gleam and shake
And flock your paths with wonder. In your gaze
Show me the vanquished vigil of my days.
Mute in that golden silence hung with green,
Come down from heaven and bring me in your eyes
Remembrance of all beauty that has been,
And stillness from the pools of Paradise.

REPRESSION OF WAR EXPERIENCE

Now light the candles; one; two; there's a moth;
What silly beggars they are to blunder in
And scorch their wings with glory, liquid flame--
No, no, not that,--it's bad to think of war,
When thoughts you've gagged all day come back to scare you;
And it's been proved that soldiers don't go mad
Unless they lose control of ugly thoughts
That drive them out to jabber among the trees.

Now light your pipe; look, what a steady hand,
Draw a deep breath; stop thinking, count fifteen,
And you're as right as rain...
                    Why won't it rain? ...
I wish there'd be a thunder-storm to-night,
With bucketsful of water to sluice the dark,
And make the roses hang their dripping heads.

Books; what a jolly company they are,
Standing so quiet and patient on their shelves,
Dressed in dim brown, and black, and white, and green,
And every kind of colour. Which will you read?
Come on; O *do* read something; they're so wise.
I tell you all the wisdom of the world
Is waiting for you on those shelves; and yet

You sit and gnaw your nails, and let your pipe out,
And listen to the silence: on the ceiling
There's one big, dizzy moth that bumps and flutters;
And in the breathless air outside the house
The garden waits for something that delays.
There must be crowds of ghosts among the trees,--
Not people killed in battle,--they're in France,--
But horrible shapes in shrouds--old men who died
Slow, natural deaths,--old men with ugly souls,
Who wore their bodies out with nasty sins.

*   *   *   *   *

You're quiet and peaceful, summering safe at home;
You'd never think there was a bloody war on! ...
O yes, you would ... why, you can hear the guns.
Hark! Thud, thud, thud,--quite soft ... they never cease--
Those whispering guns--O Christ, I want to go out
And screech at them to stop--I'm going crazy;
I'm going stark, staring mad because of the guns.

THE TRIUMPH

When life was a cobweb of stars for Beauty who came
  In the whisper of leaves or a bird's lone cry in the glen,
On dawn-lit hills and horizons girdled with flame
  I sought for the triumph that troubles the faces of men.

With death in the terrible flickering gloom of the fight
  I was cruel and fierce with despair; I was naked and bound;
  was stricken: and Beauty returned through the shambles of night;
  In the faces of men she returned; and their triumph I found.

SURVIVORS

No doubt they'll soon get well; the shock and strain
  Have caused their stammering, disconnected talk.
Of course they're "longing to go out again,"--
  These boys with old, scared faces, learning to walk,
They'll soon forget their haunted nights; their cowed
  Subjection to the ghosts of friends who died,--
Their dreams that drip with murder; and they'll be proud
  Of glorious war that shatter'd all their pride ...
Men who went out to battle, grim and glad;
Children, with eyes that hate you, broken and mad.

CRAIGLOCKART,
  Oct. 1917.

JOY-BELLS

Ring your sweet bells; but let them be farewells
  To the green-vista'd gladness of the past
That changed us into soldiers; swing your bells
  To a joyful chime; but let it be the last.

What means this metal in windy belfries hung
  When guns are all our need? Dissolve these bells
Whose tones are tuned for peace: with martial tongue
  Let them cry doom and storm the sun with shells.

Bells are like fierce-browed prelates who proclaim
  That "if our Lord returned He'd fight for *us*."
So let our bells and bishops do the same,
  Shoulder to shoulder with the motor bus.

REMORSE

Lost in the swamp and welter of the pit,
He flounders off the duck-boards; only he knows
Each flash, and spouting crash,--each instant lit
When gloom reveals the streaming rain. He goes
Heavily, blindly on. And, while he blunders,
"Could anything be worse than this!"--he wonders,
Remembering how he saw those Germans run,
Screaming for mercy among the stumps of trees:
Green-faced, they dodged and darted: there was one
Livid with terror, clutching at his knees...
Our chaps were sticking 'em like pigs... "O hell!"
He thought--"there's things in war one dare not tell
Poor father sitting safe at home, who reads
Of dying heroes and their deathless deeds."

DEAD MUSICIANS

I

From you, Beethoven, Bach, Mozart,
  The substance of my dreams took fire.
You built cathedrals in my heart,
  And lit my pinnacled desire.
You were the ardour and the bright
  Procession of my thoughts toward prayer.
You were the wrath of storm, the light
  On distant citadels aflare.

II

Great names, I cannot find you now
  In these loud years of youth that strives
Through doom toward peace: upon my brow
  I wear a wreath of banished lives.
You have no part with lads who fought
  And laughed and suffered at my side.
Your fugues and symphonies have brought
  No memory of my friends who died.

III

For when my brain is on their track,
In slangy speech I call them back.
With fox-trot tunes their ghosts I charm.
    "Another little drink won't do us any harm."
    I think of rag-time; a bit of rag-time;
    And see their faces crowding round
    To the sound of the syncopated beat.
    They've got such jolly things to tell,
    Home from hell with a Blighty wound so neat...

*   *   *   *   *

And so the song breaks off; and I'm alone.
They're dead... For God's sake stop that gramophone.

THE DREAM

I

Moonlight and dew-drenched blossom, and the scent
Of summer gardens; these can bring you all
Those dreams that in the starlit silence fall:
Sweet songs are full of odours.
                                While I went
Last night in drizzling dusk along a lane,
I passed a squalid farm; from byre and midden
Came the rank smell that brought me once again
A dream of war that in the past was hidden.

II

Up a disconsolate straggling village street
I saw the tired troops trudge: I heard their feet.
The cheery Q M.S. was there to meet
And guide our Company in ...
                                I watched them stumble
Into some crazy hovel, too beat to grumble;
Saw them file inward, slipping from their backs
Rifles, equipment, packs.
On filthy straw they sit in the gloom, each face
Bowed to patched, sodden boots they must unlace,

While the wind chills their sweat through chinks and cracks.

III

I'm looking at their blistered feet; young Jones
Stares up at me, mud-splashed and white and jaded;
Out of his eyes the morning light has faded.
Old soldiers with three winters in their bones
Puff their damp Woodbines, whistle, stretch their toes:
They can still grin at me, for each of 'em knows
That I'm as tired as they are ...
                    Can they guess
The secret burden that is always mine?--
Pride in their courage; pity for their distress;
And burning bitterness
That I must take them to the accursed Line.

IV

I cannot hear their voices, but I see
Dim candles in the barn: they gulp their tea,
And soon they'll sleep like logs. Ten miles away
The battle winks and thuds in blundering strife.
And I must lead them nearer, day by day,
To the foul beast of war that bludgeons life.

IN BARRACKS

The barrack-square, washed clean with rain,
Shines wet and wintry-grey and cold.
Young Fusiliers, strong-legged and bold,
March and wheel and march again.
The sun looks over the barrack gate,
Warm and white with glaring shine,
To watch the soldiers of the Line
That life has hired to fight with fate.

Fall out: the long parades are done.
Up comes the dark; down goes the sun.
The square is walled with windowed light.
Sleep well, you lusty Fusiliers;
Shut your brave eyes on sense and sight,
And banish from your dreamless ears
The bugle's lying notes that say,
"Another night; another day."

TOGETHER

Splashing along the boggy woods all day,
And over brambled hedge and holding clay,
I shall not think of him:
But when the watery fields grow brown and dim,
And hounds have lost their fox, and horses tire,
I know that he'll be with me on my way
Home through the darkness to the evening fire.

He's jumped each stile along the glistening lanes;
His hand will be upon the mud-soaked reins;
Hearing the saddle creak,
He'll wonder if the frost will come next week.
I shall forget him in the morning light;
And while we gallop on he will not speak:
But at the stable-door he'll say good-night.

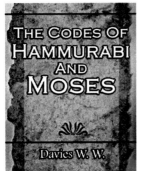

The Codes Of Hammurabi And Moses
W. W. Davies

QTY

The discovery of the Hammurabi Code is one of the greatest achievements of archaeology, and is of paramount interest, not only to the student of the Bible, but also to all those interested in ancient history...

Religion   **ISBN:** *1-59462-338-4*   **Pages:132**
MSRP $12.95

The Theory of Moral Sentiments
Adam Smith

QTY

This work from 1749. contains original theories of conscience amd moral judgment and it is the foundation for systemof morals.

Philosophy **ISBN:** *1-59462-777-0*   **Pages:536**
MSRP $19.95

Jessica's First Prayer
Hesba Stretton

QTY

In a screened and secluded corner of one of the many railway-bridges which span the streets of London there could be seen a few years ago, from five o'clock every morning until half past eight, a tidily set-out coffee-stall, consisting of a trestle and board, upon which stood two large tin cans, with a small fire of charcoal burning under each so as to keep the coffee boiling during the early hours of the morning when the work-people were thronging into the city on their way to their daily toil...

Pages:84

Childrens   **ISBN:** *1-59462-373-2*   *MSRP $9.95*

My Life and Work
Henry Ford

QTY

Henry Ford revolutionized the world with his implementation of mass production for the Model T automobile. Gain valuable business insight into his life and work with his own auto-biography... "We have only started on our development of our country we have not as yet, with all our talk of wonderful progress, done more than scratch the surface. The progress has been wonderful enough but..."

Pages:300

Biographies/   **ISBN:** *1-59462-198-5*   *MSRP $21.95*

www.bookjungle.com *email: sales@bookjungle.com fax: 630-214-0564 mail: Book Jungle PO Box 2226 Champaign, IL 61825*

The Art of Cross-Examination
Francis Wellman

I presume it is the experience of every author, after his first book is published upon an important subject, to be almost overwhelmed with a wealth of ideas and illustrations which could readily have been included in his book, and which to his own mind, at least, seem to make a second edition inevitable. Such certainly was the case with me; and when the first edition had reached its sixth impression in five months, I rejoiced to learn that it seemed to my publishers that the book had met with a sufficiently favorable reception to justify a second and considerably enlarged edition. ..

QTY

Reference   ISBN: *1-59462-647-2*   **Pages:412**   *MSRP $19.95*

On the Duty of Civil Disobedience
Henry David Thoreau

Thoreau wrote his famous essay, On the Duty of Civil Disobedience, as a protest against an unjust but popular war and the immoral but popular institution of slave-owning. He did more than write—he declined to pay his taxes, and was hauled off to gaol in consequence. Who can say how much this refusal of his hastened the end of the war and of slavery ?

QTY

Law   ISBN: *1-59462-747-9*   **Pages:48**   *MSRP $7.45*

Dream Psychology Psychoanalysis for Beginners
Sigmund Freud

Sigmund Freud, born Sigismund Schlomo Freud (May 6, 1856 - September 23, 1939), was a Jewish-Austrian neurologist and psychiatrist who co-founded the psychoanalytic school of psychology. Freud is best known for his theories of the unconscious mind, especially involving the mechanism of repression; his redefinition of sexual desire as mobile and directed towards a wide variety of objects; and his therapeutic techniques, especially his understanding of transference in the therapeutic relationship and the presumed value of dreams as sources of insight into unconscious desires.

QTY

Dream Psychology
Psychoanalysis for Beginners

Sigmund Freud

Psychology   ISBN: *1-59462-905-6*   **Pages:196**   *MSRP $15.45*

The Miracle of Right Thought
Orison Swett Marden

Believe with all of your heart that you will do what you were made to do. When the mind has once formed the habit of holding cheerful, happy, prosperous pictures, it will not be easy to form the opposite habit. It does not matter how improbable or how far away this realization may see, or how dark the prospects may be, if we visualize them as best we can, as vividly as possible, hold tenaciously to them and vigorously struggle to attain them, they will gradually become actualized, realized in the life. But a desire, a longing without endeavor, a yearning abandoned or held indifferently will vanish without realization.

QTY

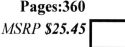

Self Help   ISBN: *1-59462-644-8*   **Pages:360**   *MSRP $25.45*

QTY

☐ **The Rosicrucian Cosmo-Conception Mystic Christianity** *by Max Heindel*   ISBN: *1-59462-188-8* **$38.95**
The Rosicrucian Cosmo-conception is not dogmatic, neither does it appeal to any other authority than the reason of the student. It is: not controversial, but is: sent forth in the, hope that it may help to clear...   New Age Religion Pages 646

☐ **Abandonment To Divine Providence** *by Jean-Pierre de Caussade*   ISBN: *1-59462-228-0* **$25.95**
"The Rev. Jean Pierre de Caussade was one of the most remarkable spiritual writers of the Society of Jesus in France in the 18th Century. His death took place at Toulouse in 1751. His works have gone through many editions and have been republished...   Inspirational Religion Pages 400

☐ **Mental Chemistry** *by Charles Haanel*   ISBN: *1-59462-192-6* **$23.95**
Mental Chemistry allows the change of material conditions by combining and appropriately utilizing the power of the mind. Much like applied chemistry creates something new and unique out of careful combinations of chemicals the mastery of mental chemistry...   New Age Pages 354

☐ **The Letters of Robert Browning and Elizabeth Barret Barrett 1845-1846 vol II**   ISBN: *1-59462-193-4* **$35.95**
by Robert Browning *and Elizabeth Barrett*   Biographies Pages 596

☐ **Gleanings In Genesis (volume I)** *by Arthur W. Pink*   ISBN: *1-59462-130-6* **$27.45**
Appropriately has Genesis been termed "the seed plot of the Bible" for in it we have, in germ form, almost all of the great doctrines which are afterwards fully developed in the books of Scripture which follow...   Religion/Inspirational Pages 420

☐ **The Master Key** *by L. W. de Laurence*   ISBN: *1-59462-001-6* **$30.95**
In no branch of human knowledge has there been a more lively increase of the spirit of research during the past few years than in the study of Psychology, Concentration and Mental Discipline. The requests for authentic lessons in Thought Control, Mental Discipline and...   New Age/Business Pages 422

☐ **The Lesser Key Of Solomon Goetia** *by L. W. de Laurence*   ISBN: *1-59462-092-X* **$9.95**
This translation of the first book of the "Lernegton" which is now for the first time made accessible to students of Talismanic Magic was done, after careful collation and edition, from numerous Ancient Manuscripts in Hebrew, Latin, and French...   New Age Occult Pages 92

☐ **Rubaiyat Of Omar Khayyam** *by Edward Fitzgerald*   ISBN: *1-59462-332-5* **$13.95**
Edward Fitzgerald, whom the world has already learned, in spite of his own efforts to remain within the shadow of anonymity, to look upon as one of the rarest poets of the century, was born at Bredfield, in Suffolk, on the 31st of March, 1809. He was the third son of John Purcell...   Music Pages 172

☐ **Ancient Law** *by Henry Maine*   ISBN: *1-59462-128-4* **$29.95**
The chief object of the following pages is to indicate some of the earliest ideas of mankind, as they are reflected in Ancient Law, and to point out the relation of those ideas to modern thought.   Religion/History Pages 452

☐ **Far-Away Stories** *by William J. Locke*   ISBN: *1-59462-129-2* **$19.45**
"Good wine needs no bush, but a collection of mixed vintages does. And this book is just such a collection. Some of the stories I do not want to remain buried for ever in the museum files of dead magazine-numbers an author's not unpardonable vanity..."   Fiction Pages 272

☐ **Life of David Crockett** *by David Crockett*   ISBN: *1-59462-250-7* **$27.45**
"Colonel David Crockett was one of the most remarkable men of the times in which he lived. Born in humble life, but gifted with a strong will, an indomitable courage, and unremitting perseverance...   Biographies/New Age Pages 424

☐ **Lip-Reading** *by Edward Nitchie*   ISBN: *1-59462-206-X* **$25.95**
Edward B. Nitchie, founder of the New York School for the Hard of Hearing, now the Nitchie School of Lip-Reading, Inc, wrote "LIP-READING Principles and Practice". The development and perfecting of this meritorious work on lip-reading was an undertaking...   How-to Pages 400

☐ **A Handbook of Suggestive Therapeutics, Applied Hypnotism, Psychic Science**   ISBN: *1-59462-214-0* **$24.95**
by Henry Munro   Health/New Age/Health/Self-help Pages 376

☐ **A Doll's House: and Two Other Plays** *by Henrik Ibsen*   ISBN: *1-59462-112-8* **$19.95**
Henrik Ibsen created this classic when in revolutionary 1848 Rome. Introducing some striking concepts in playwriting for the realist genre, this play has been studied the world over.   Fiction Classics Plays 308

☐ **The Light of Asia** *by sir Edwin Arnold*   ISBN: *1-59462-204-3* **$13.95**
In this poetic masterpiece, Edwin Arnold describes the life and teachings of Buddha. The man who was to become known as Buddha to the world was born as Prince Gautama of India but he rejected the worldly riches and abandoned the reigns of power when...   Religion/History/Biographies Pages 170

☐ **The Complete Works of Guy de Maupassant** *by Guy de Maupassant*   ISBN: *1-59462-157-8* **$16.95**
"For days and days, nights and nights, I had dreamed of that first kiss which was to consecrate our engagement, and I knew not on what spot I should put my lips..."   Fiction Classics Pages 240

☐ **The Art of Cross-Examination** *by Francis L. Wellman*   ISBN: *1-59462-309-0* **$26.95**
Written by a renowned trial lawyer, Wellman imparts his experience and uses case studies to explain how to use psychology to extract desired information through questioning.   How-to/Science/Reference Pages 408

☐ **Answered or Unanswered?** *by Louisa Vaughan*   ISBN: *1-59462-248-5* **$10.95**
Miracles of Faith in China   Religion Pages 112

☐ **The Edinburgh Lectures on Mental Science (1909)** *by Thomas*   ISBN: *1-59462-008-3* **$11.95**
This book contains the substance of a course of lectures recently given by the writer in the Queen Street Hall, Edinburgh. Its purpose is to indicate the Natural Principles governing the relation between Mental Action and Material Conditions...   New Age/Psychology Pages 148

☐ **Ayesha** *by H. Rider Haggard*   ISBN: *1-59462-301-5* **$24.95**
Verily and indeed it is the unexpected that happens! Probably if there was one person upon the earth from whom the Editor of this, and of a certain previous history, did not expect to hear again...   Classics Pages 380

☐ **Ayala's Angel** *by Anthony Trollope*   ISBN: *1-59462-352-X* **$29.95**
The two girls were both pretty, but Lucy who was twenty-one who supposed to be simple and comparatively unattractive, whereas Ayala was credited, as her Bombwhat romantic name might show, with poetic charm and a taste for romance. Ayala when her father died was nineteen...   Fiction Pages 484

☐ **The American Commonwealth** *by James Bryce*   ISBN: *1-59462-286-8* **$34.45**
An interpretation of American democratic political theory. It examines political mechanics and society from the perspective of Scotsman James Bryce   Politics Pages 572

☐ **Stories of the Pilgrims** *by Margaret P. Pumphrey*   ISBN: *1-59462-116-0* **$17.95**
This book explores pilgrims religious oppression in England as well as their escape to Holland and eventual crossing to America on the Mayflower, and their early days in New England...   History Pages 268

www.bookjungle.com *email: sales@bookjungle.com fax: 630-214-0564 mail: Book Jungle PO Box 2226 Champaign, IL 61825*

QTY

The Fasting Cure *by Sinclair Upton*
In the Cosmopolitan Magazine for May, 1910, and in the Contemporary Review (London) for April, 1910, I published an article dealing with my experiences in fasting. I have written a great many magazine articles, but never one which attracted so much attention... New Age/Self Help/Health Pages 164
ISBN: *1-59462-222-1* **$13.95**

Hebrew Astrology *by Sepharial*
In these days of advanced thinking it is a matter of common observation that we have left many of the old landmarks behind and that we are now pressing forward to greater heights and to a wider horizon than that which represented the mind-content of our progenitors... Astrology Pages 144
ISBN: *1-59462-308-2* **$13.45**

Thought Vibration or The Law of Attraction in the Thought World
by William Walker Atkinson
Psychology/Religion Pages 144
ISBN: *1-59462-127-6* **$12.95**

Optimism *by Helen Keller*
Helen Keller was blind, deaf, and mute since 19 months old, yet famously learned how to overcome these handicaps, communicate with the world, and spread her lectures promoting optimism. An inspiring read for everyone... Biographies/Inspirational Pages 84
ISBN: *1-59462-108-X* **$15.95**

Sara Crewe *by Frances Burnett*
In the first place, Miss Minchin lived in London. Her home was a large, dull, tall one, in a large, dull square, where all the houses were alike, and all the sparrows were alike, and where all the door-knockers made the same heavy sound... Childrens/Classic Pages 88
ISBN: *1-59462-360-0* **$9.45**

The Autobiography of Benjamin Franklin *by Benjamin Franklin*
The Autobiography of Benjamin Franklin has probably been more extensively read than any other American historical work, and no other book of its kind has had such ups and downs of fortune. Franklin lived for many years in England, where he was agent... Biographies/History Pages 332
ISBN: *1-59462-135-7* **$24.95**

Name	
Email	
Telephone	
Address	
City, State ZIP	

☐ **Credit Card**　　　☐ **Check / Money Order**

Credit Card Number	
Expiration Date	
Signature	

Please Mail to:　Book Jungle
PO Box 2226
Champaign, IL 61825
or Fax to:　　　630-214-0564

ORDERING INFORMATION
web: *www.bookjungle.com*
email: *sales@bookjungle.com*
fax: *630-214-0564*
mail: *Book Jungle PO Box 2226 Champaign, IL 61825*
or PayPal *to sales@bookjungle.com*

Please contact us for bulk discounts

DIRECT-ORDER TERMS

20% Discount if You Order Two or More Books
Free Domestic Shipping!
Accepted: Master Card, Visa, Discover, American Express

Lightning Source UK Ltd.
Milton Keynes UK
UKOW02f1859221013

219576UK00007B/182/P